BECOMING A FAB JUNIOR DESIGNER

CHILDREN'S FASHION BOOKS

BABY PROFESSOR

EDUCATION KIDS

Do you like to draw
and make your own
clothing designs?

It's never too early
to start designing
and learning to
become a fab
junior designer.

Kids like Melissa Jade Aeillo (age 12), Mosiah Bridges (age 11), Cecilia Cassini (age 14), and many more are known to be good designers even though they are still quite young.

How can you
become a fab
designer?

Here are some steps that you can follow:

Learn from books, magazines, and online sources about fashion and designing. Read about the biographies of fashion designers and the history of fashion.

Learn the challenges that designers encounter and how they find ways to solve those problems and pitfalls. You will find many other things you need to know on how to design fashion clothing.

Get the things
you need to make
designs. These are
sketch books and
art supplies. Be sure
to use good quality
tools and paper at
all times for you
to create good
quality drawings.

Develop your
drawing and design
skills. Even though
you are too young
to be admitted
to study in design
schools, you can still
start honing your
skills by getting
art or drawing
lessons, and by
drawing every day.

You will earn drawing techniques that will help you perfect your style of work. Inform your teachers of what you want to focus on doing or that you are hoping to become a fashion designer so they may give you more fashion-related projects.

Find inspiration in making your unique designs and don't copy what others have done. Most fashion designers are inspired by the artists who have gone before them.

They find inspiration from the work of the fashion designers they idolized, but they don't just steal their designs. Be sure to find your own expression and make styles that will stand the test of time and will make you stand out.

You can't expect
to make an
outstanding design
overnight, so allow
yourself some time
to develop your
skills. Be sure to
take note of your
own taste changes
and the things
you like so you can
refer to them at
some future time.

Improvise on existing designs. Use varied clothing, colors, and patterns to bring out your own unique and creative designs.

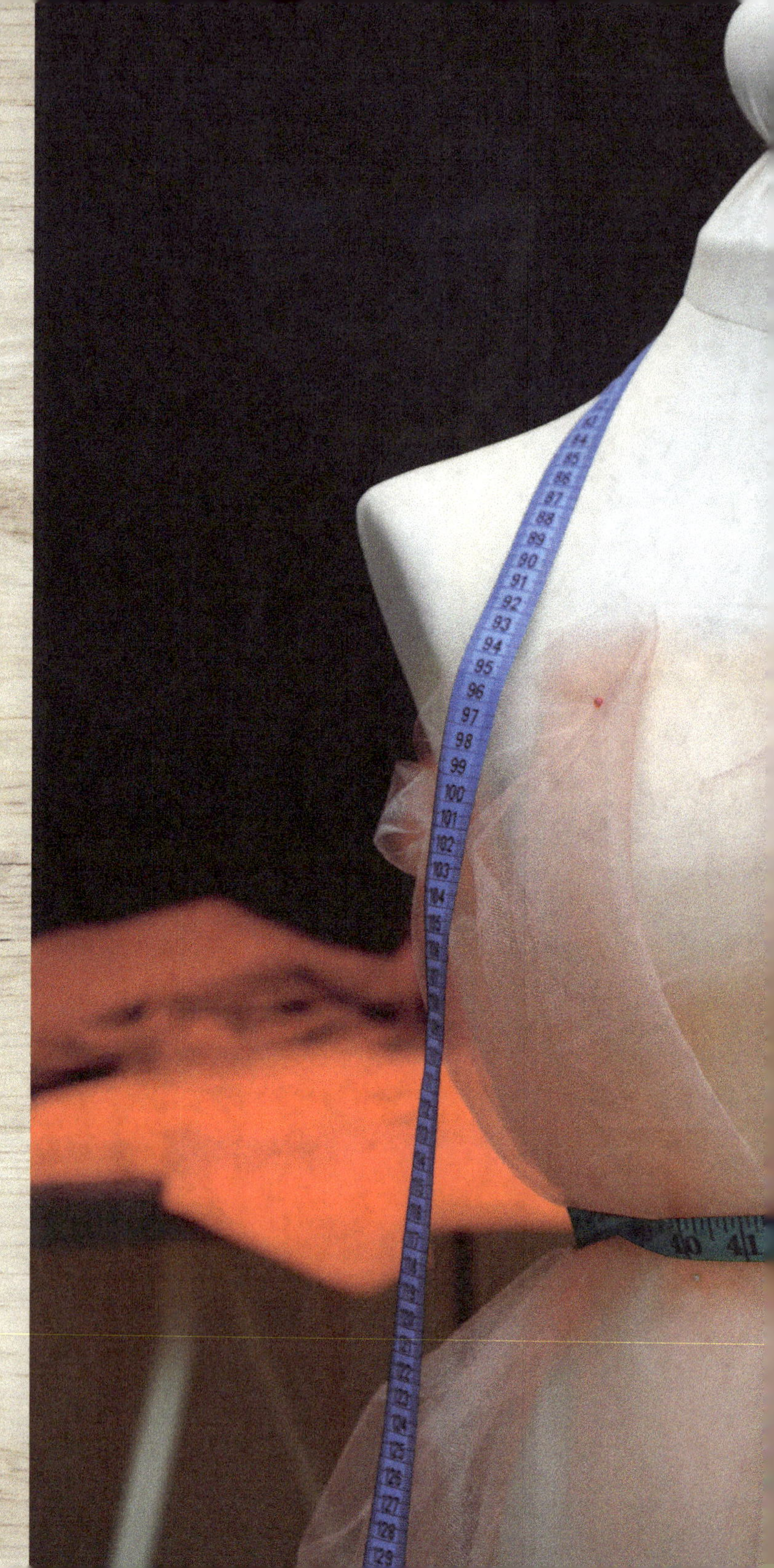

Allow yourself some room for change. Trends change with time so go with the change and make fresh designs.

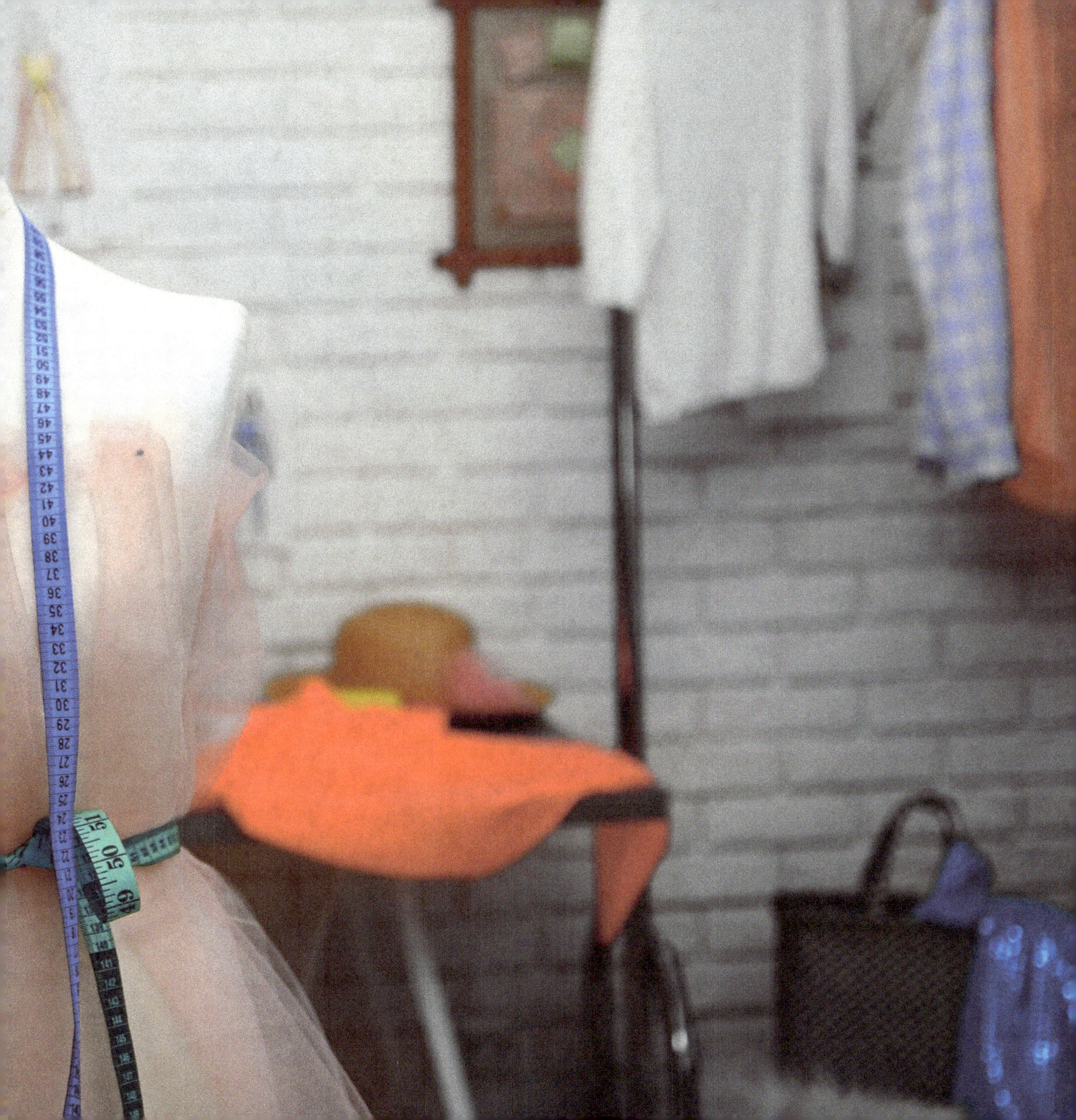

Go to fashion design studios to gain experience. Tell them you want to learn how they do their work and you can even ask them to allow you to work with them for experience.

Learn all you can about fabrics. There are different kinds of fabric. They are of man-made and natural fibers, or a mixture of the two. There are vintage and modern fabric motifs and you must decide what to use to make your design standout.

Learn the characteristics of the fabrics, like their strength, textures, and their ability to be flowing or stiff. Learn to sew. You can make more valuable designs when you know how to put things together by sewing. So learn the skill.

Be your own model!
When you think
you have a design
that is good, make
it in fabric, in the
right size for you
to wear. Then put
it on and walk
down the street, or
at least around in
your house. See how
people react to your
brand-new design!

Did you enjoy
reading this book?
Share this to
your friends.

Visit
BABY PROFESSOR
EDUCATION KIDS
www.BabyProfessorBooks.com
to download Free Baby Professor eBooks
and view our catalog of new and exciting
Children's Books